Poems of 1

GW01048614

Poems of 1912–13

THOMAS HARDY

Preface by DONALD DAVIE

SYRENS

THOMAS HARDY 1840–1928

S Y R E N S Published by the Penguin Group. Penguin Books Ltd, 27 Wrights Lane, London w8 5tz, England. Penguin Books USA Inc., 375 Hudson Street, New York, New York 10014, USA. Penguin Books Australia Ltd, Ringwood, Victoria, Australia. Penguin Books Canada Ltd, 10 Alcorn Avenue, Toronto, Ontario, Canada m4v 3b2. Penguin Books (NZ) Ltd, 182–190 Wairau Road, Auckland 10, New Zealand. Penguin Books Ltd, Registered Offices: Harmondsworth, Middlesex, England. Published in Syrens 1995. Preface copyright © Donald Davie, 1995. All rights reserved. The moral right of the editor has been asserted. Except in the United States of America, this book is sold subject to the condition that it shall not, by way of trade or otherwise, be lent, re-sold, hired out, or otherwise circulated without the publisher's prior consent in any form of binding or cover other than that in which it is published and without a similar condition including this condition being imposed on the subsequent purchaser. Set in 9/12 pt Monotype Bembo by Datix International Limited, Bungay, Suffolk. Printed and bound by Page Bros., Norwich.   1   2   3   4   5   6   7   8   9   10

CONTENTS

PREFACE

When Hardy's novels *Tess of the D'Urbervilles* (1891) and *Jude the Obscure* (1896) provoked a moralistic hubbub, their author lost whatever faith he had in the good sense and fair-mindedness of his public. Accordingly, in what seemed a new career as poet not novelist, he played hide and seek with his readers, hiding from them those of his compositions that would lay him open to their spite. Thus he concealed his most intimate and monumental sequence of poems under the dry title 'Poems of 1912–13' and buried this in the midst of a collection which seemed to advertise by its title – *Satires of Circumstance, Lyrics and Reveries* (1914) – how heterogeneous it was, how far from being put together according to any design.

Hardy's perverse strategy worked; and it was only many years later, long after his death in 1928, that this sequence of 18 poems (later extended to 21) was recognized as indeed monumental. Yet Hardy had planted a clue which should have been seized on from the first: the Latin epigraph, '*Veteris vestigia flammae*', from Virgil's *Aeneid* (IV, 23). Hardy's first wife, Emma, with whom he continued to co-habit, though they had long been estranged, had died, suddenly and for the poet unexpectedly, in 1912. By 1913, Hardy was already involved with Florence Emily Dugdale, whom in the next year he was to take as his second wife. There is an obvious correlation between this situation in Hardy's life and the epigraph, for the excerpted phrase ('ashes of an old fire') is at the heart of the confession by Dido, Queen of Carthage, that the love she had felt for her dead husband Sychaeus is about to renew itself for the vagabond visitor to her court, Aeneas. Virgil tells how Dido's love for Aeneas was indeed consummated; how Aeneas abandoned her; and how in the underworld (Book VI) Dido's shade, now reunited with Sychaeus, haughtily spurns her faithless lover. The modern poet, guiltily reminiscent and apprehensive, between one ill-used wife lately dead and another too promptly wooed, sees his situation foreshadowed in the ancient masterpiece. This does not excuse his predicament, but it dignifies it, by giving it such an illustrious precedent. Moreover, he lets Virgil's precedent dictate the order of the sequence, which can be seen to re-enact Aeneas's descent to the underworld, in so far as it charts a sort of penitential pilgrimage that Hardy undertook in 1912 and 1913 from the Dorsetshire home he had built, where Emma had died, to the North Cornwall where he had courted her years before, and back by way of Plymouth, where Emma had grown up. By carefully dating most of the poems, and tellingly locating some of them (in Pentargan Bay, Beeny Cliff, Plymouth), Hardy invites this reading, even as he ensures that only a few attentive readers will accept the invitation.

Not everyone will welcome this evidence that Hardy could proceed as did his contemporary James Joyce, who in his *Ulysses* tied a narrative of one day in Edwardian Dublin to the ancient precedent of Homer's *Odyssey*. Too often even today Hardy is loved for supposedly being direct and artlessly frank with his readers, as Joyce and T. S. Eliot were not. But this is far from the truth. Hardy, a very accomplished Latinist, uses Virgil's Latin to shield his face when he directs the blowtorch of his poetry into especially flammable corners of his experience. Shielded thus, he is able to discern and declare that the identity of a human person,

and the quality of experience known to that person,
persist metaphysically after that person's death.

Donald Davie

Poems of 1912–13

Veteris vestigia flammae

The Going

Why did you give no hint that night
That quickly, after the morrow's dawn,
And calmly, as if indifferent quite,
You would close your term here, up and be gone
        Where I could not follow
        With wing of swallow
To gain one glimpse of you ever anon!

        Never to bid good-bye,
        Or lip me the softest call,
Or utter a wish for a word, while I
Saw morning harden upon the wall,
        Unmoved, unknowing
        That your great going
Had place that moment, and altered all.

Why do you make me leave the house
And think for a breath it is you I see
At the end of the alley of bending boughs
Where so often at dusk you used to be;
        Till in darkening dankness
        The yawning blankness
Of the perspective sickens me!

You were she who abode
         By those red-veined rocks far West,
You were the swan-necked one who rode
Along the beetling Beèny Crest,
         And, reining nigh me,
         Would muse and eye me,
While Life unrolled us its very best.

Why, then, latterly did we not speak,
Did we not think of those days long dead,
And ere your vanishing strive to seek
That time's renewal? We might have said,
         'In this bright spring weather
         We'll visit together
Those places that once we visited.'

         Well, well! All's past amend,
         Unchangeable. It must go.
I seem but a dead man held on end
To sink down soon . . . O you could not know
         That such swift fleeing
         No soul foreseeing –
Not even I – would undo me so!

December 1912

Your Last Drive

Here by the moorway you returned,
And saw the borough lights ahead
That lit your face – all undiscerned
To be in a week the face of the dead,
And you told of the charm of that haloed view
That never again would beam on you.

And on your left you passed the spot
Where eight days later you were to lie,
And be spoken of as one who was not;
Beholding it with a heedless eye
As alien from you, though under its tree
You soon would halt everlastingly.

I drove not with you . . . Yet had I sat
At your side that eve I should not have seen
That the countenance I was glancing at
Had a last-time look in the flickering sheen,
Nor have read the writing upon your face,
'I go hence soon to my resting-place;

'You may miss me then. But I shall not know
How many times you visit me there,
Or what your thoughts are, or if you go
There never at all. And I shall not care.
Should you censure me I shall take no heed,
And even your praises no more shall need.'

True: never you'll know. And you will not mind.
But shall I then slight you because of such?
Dear ghost, in the past did you ever find
The thought 'What profit,' move me much?
Yet abides the fact, indeed, the same, –
You are past love, praise, indifference, blame.

December 1912

The Walk

You did not walk with me
Of late to the hill-top tree
    By the gated ways,
    As in earlier days;
    You were weak and lame,
    So you never came,
And I went alone, and I did not mind,
Not thinking of you as left behind.

I walked up there to-day
Just in the former way;
    Surveyed around
    The familiar ground
    By myself again:
    What difference, then?
Only that underlying sense
Of the look of a room on returning thence.

Rain on a Grave

Clouds spout upon her
  Their waters amain
  In ruthless disdain, –
Her who but lately
  Had shivered with pain
As at touch of dishonour
If there had lit on her
So coldly, so straightly
  Such arrows of rain:

One who to shelter
  Her delicate head
Would quicken and quicken
  Each tentative tread
If drops chanced to pelt her
  That summertime spills
  In dust-paven rills
When thunder-clouds thicken
  And birds close their bills.

Would that I lay there
     And she were housed here!
Or better, together
Were folded away there
Exposed to one weather
We both, – who would stray there
When sunny the day there,
     Or evening was clear
     At the prime of the year.

Soon will be growing
     Green blades from her mound,
And daisies be showing
     Like stars on the ground,
Till she form part of them –
Ay – the sweet heart of them,
Loved beyond measure
With a child's pleasure
   All her life's round.

31 January 1913

'I Found Her Out There'

I found her out there
On a slope few see,
That falls westwardly
To the salt-edged air,
Where the ocean breaks
On the purple strand,
And the hurricane shakes
The solid land.

I brought her here,
And have laid her to rest
In a noiseless nest
No sea beats near.
She will never be stirred
In her loamy cell
By the waves long heard
And loved so well.

So she does not sleep
By those haunted heights
The Atlantic smites
And the blind gales sweep,

Whence she often would gaze
At Dundagel's famed head,
While the dipping blaze
Dyed her face fire-red;

And would sigh at the tale
Of sunk Lyonnesse,
As a wind-tugged tress
Flapped her cheek like a flail;
Or listen at whiles
With a thought-bound brow
To the murmuring miles
She is far from now.

Yet her shade, maybe,
Will creep underground
Till it catch the sound
Of that western sea
As it swells and sobs
Where she once domiciled,
And joy in its throbs
With the heart of a child.

Without Ceremony

It was your way, my dear,
To vanish without a word
When callers, friends, or kin
Had left, and I hastened in
To rejoin you, as I inferred.

And when you'd a mind to career
Off anywhere – say to town –
You were all on a sudden gone
Before I had thought thereon,
Or noticed your trunks were down.

So, now that you disappear
For ever in that swift style,
Your meaning seems to me
Just as it used to be:
'Good-bye is not worth while!'

Lament

How she would have loved
A party to-day! –
Bright-hatted and gloved,
With table and tray
And chairs on the lawn
Her smiles would have shone
With welcomings . . . But
She is shut, she is shut
     From friendship's spell
     In the jailing shell
     Of her tiny cell.

Or she would have reigned
At a dinner to-night
With ardours unfeigned,
And a generous delight:
All in her abode
She'd have freely bestowed
On her guests . . . But alas,
She is shut under grass
     Where no cups flow,
     Powerless to know
     That it might be so.

And she would have sought
With a child's eager glance
The shy snowdrops brought
By the new year's advance,
And peered in the rime
Of Candlemas-time
For crocuses . . . chanced
It that she were not tranced
      From sights she loved best;
      Wholly possessed
      By an infinite rest!

And we are here staying
Amid these stale things,
Who care not for gaying,
And those junketings
That used so to joy her,
And never to cloy her
As us they cloy! . . . But
She is shut, she is shut
      From the cheer of them, dead
      To all done and said
      In her yew-arched bed.

The Haunter

He does not think that I haunt here nightly:
      How shall I let him know
That whither his fancy sets him wandering
      I, too, alertly go? –
Hover and hover a few feet from him
      Just as I used to do,
But cannot answer the words he lifts me –
      Only listen thereto!

When I could answer he did not say them:
      When I could let him know
How I would like to join in his journeys
      Seldom he wished to go.
Now that he goes and wants me with him
      More than he used to do,
Never he sees my faithful phantom
      Though he speaks thereto.

Yes, I companion him to places
      Only dreamers know,
Where the shy hares print long paces,
      Where the night rooks go;

Into old aisles where the past is all to him,
   Close as his shade can do,
Always lacking the power to call to him,
   Near as I reach thereto!

What a good haunter I am, O tell him!
   Quickly make him know
If he but sigh since my loss befell him
   Straight to his side I go.
Tell him a faithful one is doing
   All that love can do
Still that his path may be worth pursuing,
   And to bring peace thereto.

The Voice

Woman much missed, how you call to me, call to me,
Saying that now you are not as you were
When you had changed from the one who was all to
    me,
But as at first, when our day was fair.

Can it be you that I hear? Let me view you, then,
Standing as when I drew near to the town
Where you would wait for me: yes, as I knew you
    then,
Even to the original air-blue gown!

Or is it only the breeze, in its listlessness
Travelling across the wet mead to me here,
You being ever dissolved to wan wistlessness,
Heard no more again far or near?

        Thus I; faltering forward,
        Leaves around me falling,
Wind oozing thin through the thorn from norward,
        And the woman calling.

December 1912

His Visitor

I come across from Mellstock while the moon wastes
     weaker
To behold where I lived with you for twenty years and
     more:
I shall go in the gray, at the passing of the mail-train,
And need no setting open of the long familiar door
               As before.

The change I notice in my once own quarters!
A formal-fashioned border where the daisies used to
     be,
The rooms new painted, and the pictures altered,
And other cups and saucers, and no cosy nook for tea
               As with me.

I discern the dim faces of the sleep-wrapt servants;
They are not those who tended me through feeble
     hours and strong,
But strangers quite, who never knew my rule here,
Who never saw me painting, never heard my softling
     song
               Float along.

So I don't want to linger in this re-decked dwelling,
I feel too uneasy at the contrasts I behold,
And I make again for Mellstock to return here never,
And rejoin the roomy silence, and the mute and
    manifold
        Souls of old.

                        1913

A Circular

As 'legal representative'
I read a missive not my own,
On new designs the senders give
    For clothes, in tints as shown.

Here figure blouses, gowns for tea,
And presentation-trains of state,
Charming ball-dresses, millinery,
    Warranted up to date.

And this gay-pictured, spring-time shout
Of Fashion, hails what lady proud?
Her who before last year ebbed out
    Was costumed in a shroud.

A Dream or No

Why go to Saint-Juliot? What's Juliot to me?
      Some strange necromancy
      But charmed me to fancy
That much of my life claims the spot as its key.

Yes. I have had dreams of that place in the West,
      And a maiden abiding
      Thereat as in hiding;
Fair-eyed and white-shouldered, broad-browed and
    brown-tressed.

And of how, coastward bound on a night long ago,
      There lonely I found her,
      The sea-birds around her,
And other than nigh things uncaring to know.

So sweet her life there (in my thought has it seemed)
      That quickly she drew me
      To take her unto me,
And lodge her long years with me. Such have I
    dreamed.

But nought of that maid from Saint-Juliot I see;
      Can she ever have been here,
      And shed her life's sheen here,
The woman I thought a long housemate with me?

Does there even a place like Saint-Juliot exist?
      Or a Vallency Valley
      With stream and leafed alley,
Or Beeny, or Bos with its flounce flinging mist?

February 1913

After a Journey

Hereto I come to view a voiceless ghost;
     Whither, O whither will its whim now draw
                                      me?
Up the cliff, down, till I'm lonely, lost,
     And the unseen waters' ejaculations awe me.
Where you will next be there's no knowing,
       Facing round about me everywhere,
         With your nut-coloured hair,
And gray eyes, and rose-flush coming and going.

Yes: I have re-entered your olden haunts at last;
     Through the years, through the dead scenes I
                         have tracked you;
What have you now found to say of our past –
     Scanned across the dark space wherein I have
                        lacked you?
Summer gave us sweets, but autumn wrought division?
     Things were not lastly as firstly well
       With us twain, you tell?
But all's closed now, despite Time's derision.

I see what you are doing: you are leading me on
    To the spots we knew when we haunted here
                  together,
The waterfall, above which the mist-bow shone
    At the then fair hour in the then fair weather,
And the cave just under, with a voice still so hollow
    That it seems to call out to me from forty years
                  ago,
      When you were all aglow,
And not the thin ghost that I now frailly follow!

Ignorant of what there is flitting here to see,
    The waked birds preen and the seals flop lazily,
Soon you will have, Dear, to vanish from me,
    For the stars close their shutters and the dawn
                whitens hazily.
Trust me, I mind not, though Life lours,
    The bringing me here; nay, bring me here again!
    I am just the same as when
Our days were a joy, and our paths through flowers.

PENTARGAN BAY

A Death-Day Recalled

Beeny did not quiver,
    Juliot grew not gray,
Thin Vallency's river
    Held its wonted way.
Bos seemed not to utter
    Dimmest note of dirge,
Targan mouth a mutter
    To its creamy surge.

Yet though these, unheeding,
    Listless, passed the hour
Of her spirit's speeding,
    She had, in her flower,
Sought and loved the places –
    Much and often pined
For their lonely faces
    When in towns confined.

Why did not Vallency
    In his purl deplore
One whose haunts were whence he
    Drew his limpid store?

Why did Bos not thunder,
    Targan apprehend
Body and Breath were sunder
    Of their former friend?

Beeny Cliff

MARCH 1870–MARCH 1913

I

O the opal and the sapphire of that wandering western
    sea,

And the woman riding high above with bright hair
    flapping free –

The woman whom I loved so, and who loyally loved
    me.

II

The pale mews plained below us, and the waves seemed
    far away

In a nether sky, engrossed in saying their ceaseless
    babbling say,

As we laughed light-heartedly aloft on that clear-sunned
    March day.

III

A little cloud then cloaked us, and there flew an irised rain,

And the Atlantic dyed its levels with a dull misfeatured
stain,

And then the sun burst out again, and purples prinked
the main.

IV

– Still in all its chasmal beauty bulks old Beeny to the
sky,

And shall she and I not go there once again now
March is nigh,

And the sweet things said in that March say anew there
by and by?

V

What if still in chasmal beauty looms that wild weird
western shore,

The woman now is – elsewhere – whom the ambling
pony bore,

And nor knows nor cares for Beeny, and will laugh
there nevermore.

At Castle Boterel

As I drive to the junction of lane and highway,
        And the drizzle bedrenches the waggonette,
I look behind at the fading byway,
        And see on its slope, now glistening wet,
            Distinctly yet

Myself and a girlish form benighted
        In dry March weather. We climb the road
Beside a chaise. We had just alighted
        To ease the sturdy pony's load
            When he sighed and slowed.

What we did as we climbed, and what we talked of
        Matters not much, nor to what it led, –
Something that life will not be balked of
        Without rude reason till hope is dead,
            And feeling fled.

It filled but a minute. But was there ever
        A time of such quality, since or before,
In that hill's story? To one mind never,
        Though it has been climbed, foot-swift,
                                foot-sore,
            By thousands more.

Primaeval rocks form the road's steep border,
      And much have they faced there, first and last,
Of the transitory in Earth's long order;
        But what they record in colour and cast
          Is – that we two passed.

And to me, though Time's unflinching rigour,
      In mindless rote, has ruled from sight
The substance now, one phantom figure
        Remains on the slope, as when that night
          Saw us alight.

I look and see it there, shrinking, shrinking,
      I look back at it amid the rain
For the very last time; for my sand is sinking,
        And I shall traverse old love's domain
          Never again.

March 1913

Places

Nobody says: Ah, that is the place
Where chanced, in the hollow of years ago,
What none of the Three Towns cared to know –
The birth of a little girl of grace –
The sweetest the house saw, first or last;
        Yet it was so
        On that day long past.

Nobody thinks: There, there she lay
In a room by the Hoe, like the bud of a flower,
And listened, just after the bedtime hour,
To the stammering chimes that used to play
The quaint Old Hundred-and-Thirteenth tune
        In Saint Andrew's tower
        Night, morn, and noon.

Nobody calls to mind that here
Upon Boterel Hill, where the waggoners skid,
With cheeks whose airy flush outbid
Fresh fruit in bloom, and free of fear,
She cantered down, as if she must fall
        (Though she never did),
        To the charm of all.

Nay: one there is to whom these things,
That nobody else's mind calls back,
Have a savour that scenes in being lack,
And a presence more than the actual brings;
To whom to-day is beneaped and stale,
        And its urgent clack
        But a vapid tale.

PLYMOUTH, March 1913

The Phantom Horsewoman

I

Queer are the ways of a man I know:

> He comes and stands
> In a careworn craze,
> And looks at the sands
> And the seaward haze
> With moveless hands
> And face and gaze,
> Then turns to go . . .

And what does he see when he gazes so?

II

They say he sees as an instant thing

> More clear than to-day,
> A sweet soft scene
> That once was in play
> By that briny green;
> Yes, notes alway
> Warm, real, and keen,
> What his back years bring –

A phantom of his own figuring.

III

Of this vision of his they might say more:

Not only there
Does he see this sight,
But everywhere
In his brain – day, night,
As if on the air
It were drawn rose bright –
Yea, far from that shore

Does he carry this vision of heretofore:

IV

A ghost-girl-rider. And though, toil-tried,

He withers daily,
Time touches her not,
But she still rides gaily
In his rapt thought
On that shagged and shaly
Atlantic spot,
And as when first eyed

Draws rein and sings to the swing of the tide.

1913

The original 'Poems of 1912–13' sequence ended here, when it was first published in *Satires of Circumstance, Lyrics and Reveries* (1914). Hardy added the following three poems from the 'Lyrics and Reveries' section in *Collected Poems* (1919).

The Spell of the Rose

'I mean to build a hall anon,
    And shape two turrets there,
    And a broad newelled stair,
And a cool well for crystal water;
    Yes; I will build a hall anon,
    Plant roses love shall feed upon,
    And apple-trees and pear.'

He set to build the manor-hall,
    And shaped the turrets there,
    And the broad newelled stair,
And the cool well for crystal water;
    He built for me that manor-hall,
    And planted many trees withal,
    But no rose anywhere.

And as he planted never a rose
    That bears the flower of love,
    Though other flowers throve
Some heart-bane moved our souls to sever
    Since he had planted never a rose;
    And misconceits raised horrid shows,
    And agonies came thereof.

'I'll mend these miseries,' then said I,
        And so, at dead of night,
        I went and, screened from sight,
That nought should keep our souls in severance,
        I set a rose-bush. 'This,' said I,
        'May end divisions dire and wry,
            And long-drawn days of blight.'

    But I was called from earth – yea, called
        Before my rose-bush grew;
        And would that now I knew
What feels he of the tree I planted,
        And whether, after I was called
        To be a ghost, he, as of old,
            Gave me his heart anew!

    Perhaps now blooms that queen of trees
        I set but saw not grow,
        And he, beside its glow –
Eyes couched of the mis-vision that blurred me –
        Ay, there beside that queen of trees
        He sees me as I was, though sees
            Too late to tell me so!

St Launce's Revisited

　　Slip back, Time!
Yet again I am nearing
Castle and keep, uprearing
　　Gray, as in my prime.

　　At the inn
Smiling nigh, why is it
Not as on my visit
　　When hope and I were twin?

　　Groom and jade
Whom I found here, moulder;
Strange the tavern-holder,
　　Strange the tap-maid.

　　Here I hired
Horse and man for bearing
Me on my wayfaring
　　To the door desired.

    Evening gloomed
As I journeyed forward
To the faces shoreward,
        Till their dwelling loomed.

    If again
Towards the Atlantic sea there
I should speed, they'd be there
        Surely now as then? . . .

    Why waste thought,
When I know them vanished
Under earth; yea, banished
        Ever into nought!

Where the Picnic Was

Where we made the fire
In the summer time
Of branch and briar
On the hill to the sea,
I slowly climb
Through winter mire,
And scan and trace
The forsaken place
Quite readily.

Now a cold wind blows,
And the grass is gray,
But the spot still shows
As a burnt circle – aye,
And stick-ends, charred,
Still strew the sward
Whereon I stand,
Last relic of the band
Who came that day!

Yes, I am here
Just as last year,
And the sea breathes brine
From its strange straight line
Up hither, the same
As when we four came.
– But two have wandered far
From this grassy rise
Into urban roar
Where no picnics are,
And one – has shut her eyes
For evermore.

Kisses.

Bisous.

Love and kisses.

Tendres baisers.

Forever and for always.

Pour toujours et à jamais.

Yours forever.

A toi pour toujours.

bound in England by www.printondemand-worldwide.com

PEFC Certified

This product is
from sustainably
managed forests
and controlled
sources

www.pefc.org

C materials for the cover and PEFC materials for the text pages.

ss - Printed on 30-Jun-18 12:04